MAKE IT HAPPEN, GIRL!

YOUR POWERFUL GUIDE TO SETTING GOALS, PLANNING EFFECTIVELY, AND ACHIEVING EVERYTHING YOU WANT

FlyingKids® Presents

MAKE IT HAPPEN, GIRL!

A Girl's Guide to Setting Goals, Planning Effectively, and Achieving Everything You Want

Author:
Shira Halperin

Editor:
Carma Graber

Designer:
Nebojsa Dolovacki

Illustrations:
Oksana Melnychuk, Aaron Benjamin De Castro

Published by FlyingKids® Limited, 2022

Visit us: www.theflyingkids.com
Contact us: leonardo@theflyingkids.com
ISBN: 978-1-910994-47-4
Copyright © 2022 Shira Halperin and FlyingKids® Limited

TABLE OF CONTENTS

INTRODUCTION

> A girl should be two things: who and what she wants.
>
> — *Coco Chanel*

LIRI HERE!

Great to meet you again!

If you remember me from the first book, You Can Be Whatever You Want, Girl!, that's awesome!

If we didn't meet in my first book, I'm so glad you're here now!

I used to be the shy girl. I used to think that everyone around me was smarter and more successful than me. When I was younger, I was always doubting myself. I didn't have much confidence to try new things, whether it was new experiences or meeting new people.

I had dreams. I WANTED TO DO THINGS, but I wasn't sure I could—or even how to start.

BUT I DECIDED TO CHANGE!

Then slowly, step-by-step, **I learned to change the things** that had bothered me for as long as I could remember. After awhile, some of the things that had seemed so scary **didn't seem that scary anymore**.

I made new **friends** and tried new **things**. I learned how to **feel good** about the things that used to bother me, and I learned how to **go after things I wanted** in life, even if they felt a little bit intimidating.

You're probably asking yourself—HOW? How did I make this change?

I did it by learning about myself and discovering a few tricks and tools that helped me. And I developed my own unique set of TOOLS that are helping me every day. I showed you some of them in my first book.

Now, I want to share with you, Girl, how you can level up your skills by focusing on the most important thing that can make a big change in your life.

The thing that makes the difference between **a dreamer** and **an achiever...**

The thing that makes the difference between **a frustrated, unsuccessful girl** who feels way behind and **a girl who gets the most out of her life**!

What made the difference for me and helped me most is developing the ability to set GOALS, to build a good PLAN, and to use this plan to **ACHIEVE MY DREAMS**. And that is what we're going to focus on in this book!

This book is all about

SETTING GOALS

MAKING A WISE AND
POWERFUL PLAN

LEARNING HOW TO
ACHIEVE YOUR GOALS!

It may sound a little frightening or maybe too complicated, but don't worry! I will teach you how to use an awesome tool—the MAKE-IT-HAPPEN tool—that will make everything much easier and clearer. And I have plenty of tips for you. Of course, we'll practice until everything goes smoothly and you're able to do it like a pro!

I BELIEVE IN YOU, GIRL! I BELIEVE YOU CAN DO IT!

Just like the first book, this book is an INVITATION for a journey—the journey of making your dreams come true and achieving the goals in your life.

I invite you to step in, my dear friend, and start the journey with me.

This will be an adventure in feeling good about yourself and making yourself into an even **MORE AMAZING YOUNG WOMAN!**

This journey and this guidebook are dedicated to YOU, Girl! There is so much to learn—and it will be full of

INSPIRING THOUGHTS   HELDFUL TIPS   PRACTICAL TOOLS

I truly believe this book can help ANYONE, especially GIRLS filled with hopes and dreams! And especially you!

> ## EVERYONE'S DREAM CAN COME TRUE IF YOU JUST STICK TO IT AND WORK HARD.
>
> — *Serena Williams, American tennis player*

Part 1

WHAT ARE GOALS, AND WHY DO YOU NEED THEM?

> "If you want to live a happy life, tie it to a goal, not to people or things.
>
> — **Albert Einstein, theoretical physicist**

When I was a little girl, I used to dream about being a ballerina! And after that, I dreamt of being a dolphin trainer. Then a few years later, I had a big dream to win an Oscar (I wasn't really sure in which category, I just knew I wanted one). Since then, **my plans have changed**, and now my dream is to become a best-selling writer.

Here's a question for you. Does the fact that I used to and still do have big dreams for the future actually help me achieve them?
Hmm ... nope, I don't think so.

Dreaming about something and **wanting** it will not Make It Happen, Girl—no matter how much you actually want it. Instead, you need **clear steps** for making the dream a reality. **That's where goals come into the picture.**

You need to have a clear goal for what you wish to achieve! And then you NEED A PLAN—a plan that will help you achieve it.

GOALS ARE ALL THE THINGS YOU WANT TO ACCOMPLISH IN YOUR LIFE.

They can be large and challenging goals, or they can be smaller and more personal. It all depends on what you want to achieve.

So, why do you need goals in your life? And why isn't dreaming about them enough?

The answer is that having goals

- Helps you be more focused
- Acts as a powerful motivator
- Helps you prioritize
- And helps you with decision making

*Remember Sarah and Taylor, my friends I told you about in my first book—*You Can Be Whatever You Want, Girl!*? They were both naturally talented in sports, especially running. Recently, they both had the same GOAL—to win the national running championship. I asked both of them what their PLAN was. Exactly how did they intend to achieve their goal?*

Sarah answered: "Well, I plan to work hard and do whatever I can!"

Taylor answered: "I plan to exercise for an hour every morning before school, join the school track team, and use a professional coach. Then I'll apply to be accepted on the county track team."

So ... who do you think has the best chance of achieving her goal, Sarah or Taylor?

A GOAL WITHOUT A PLAN IS JUST A WISH.

— Antoine de Saint-Exupéry, French author of **The Little Prince**

Goals can be **simple** as "learn how to cook a nice breakfast" or as **challenging** as "learn to speak a foreign language fluently." Goals can be **large** or **small**. Sometimes it can be really hard to know **exactly what it is you want**, but have no fear! That's totally OK because, with a little assistance and a few simple tools and self-help tips, **you can figure it out**. And I'm going to teach you everything that I know in this book.

> BUT I want you to know something NOW. YOU can make YOUR DREAMS COME TRUE! YOU CAN do it—you CAN BE ANYTHING you want.

Tell yourself that now. **Shout it from the rooftops** if you want to. You can **MAKE YOUR DREAMS COME TRUE!** You CAN do it, and you CAN BE ANYTHING you desire. How good does that feel?

Now write it here. A FEW TIMES.

**I CAN MAKE MY DREAMS COME TRUE!
I CAN DO IT!**

There are many little girls who have achieved their big dreams, becoming astronauts, pediatricians, models, and so much more. There's even one little girl who became the Vice President of the United States! **All of these little girls encountered some difficulties along the way**, and for sure, it didn't happen overnight. But they all **worked hard** and **didn't give up** until they reached their goal.

AND GIRL, YOU CAN TOO!

I wrote this book for you, and I know it can help you. Girl, I'm here for you, and I'm so excited to see what you become!

OK, let's do a little exercise that can help you get clearer about your goals.

What's a behavior you'd like to **STOP DOING**?

What's a behavior you'd like to **START DOING**?

What's something new that you'd like to **TRY**?

What's something new that you'd like to **LEARN**?

> ## IF YOU AIM FOR NOTHING, YOU'LL HIT IT EVERY TIME.
>
> — *Unknown*

See you in the next chapter! ➡

Part 2

LONG- VS SHORT-TERM GOALS—AND WHY YOU NEED BOTH

> The journey of a thousand miles begins with a single step.
>
> — *Lao Tzu, Chinese philosopher and writer*

Girl, are you ready for me to share some knowledge with you? It's time to talk about the two types of goals—your LONG-TERM and SHORT-TERM goals.

In the past years, I have been focused and motivated toward the things I want, and do you know why? It's because I have **both long-term and short-term goals.** I once told you that you are unique and you have your own goal to achieve, remember? But did you know that none of this is possible without your short- and long-term goals? Yes, you need them both.

OK, let's make it clearer.

WHAT'S THE DIFFERENCE BETWEEN THE TWO TYPES OF GOALS?

There is one key difference between short-term goals and long-term goals— the TIMELINE.

SHORT-TERM goals can usually be reached in a few days, weeks, or months. LONG-TERM goals can take more time, sometimes years or more, to achieve.

WHY DO WE NEED TWO TYPES OF GOALS?

When setting goals, it's important to start with your **long-term goal**. That way, you can figure out what short-term goals you're going to need in order to achieve the long-term goal.

Think of your long-term goal as the ultimate destination you want to reach and the short-term goals as **being the steps along the way**.

Once you have your long-term goal, set the **short-term goals that will help you reach it**. That means your long-term goals can, and should, be made up of **many short-term goals and tasks**.

You can think of your short-term goals as the INGREDIENTS that make up your long-term goal.

Take, for example, Lena's story …

Lena is a fourteen-year-old girl. We know that in order to achieve her dreams, Lena must have both long- and short-term goals. Let's look at what Lena wanted to achieve. She decided that when she grew up, *she wanted to be a doctor*—a very qualified doctor. Go, Lena! Knowing that was what she wanted, Lena devised a plan to reach her long-term goal. *She scribbled her short-term goals on a sheet of paper and checked them off as they were accomplished.*

Here's what her to-do list looked like:

- Get good scores in school.
- Attend school lectures.
- Find a fantastic coach to assist me in my studies.

In the end, it all worked! And in just a few years, with much hard work, she became a doctor! That isn't to say that it was always easy. At one point, she had to retake two exams—and sure, she felt like giving up. But her end goal was far too important, and so she kept going and got there in the end. Her short aims, which she had checked off along the way, led to her becoming a qualified doctor. Goal achieved!

LONG-TERM GOALS are important because they help you FOCUS YOUR ENERGY AND RESOURCES. They also provide a guide for what you need to do in the present moment. **Without a long-term plan, it's easy to get distracted** by the things that are happening right now and to only focus on each day, instead of seeing things as a whole.

SHORT-TERM GOALS are important because they ensure that you're making progress on your BIGGER GOALS, keeping you on track. Short-term goals will also help to make your long-term goal **feel that much more achievable** because you'll be slowly chipping away at it. And short-term goals will encourage you to keep going, because ticking them off will let you experience the **taste of success much more quickly**!

Part 3

YOUR LONG-TERM GOALS

> *Planning is bringing the future into the present so that you can do something about it now.*
>
> — *Alan Lakein, American author*

I know … when you're a teenager, it can be hard **to figure out what your long-term goals are**. After all, your life is full of uncertainty and change—what you **want now may not be what you want in five years**. Girl, I get it.

And I know that it's easy to get distracted by things that take all your attention. There are **so many things happening in your life**, from extracurricular activities to relationships to school, and you probably want to make sure you're doing OK in all areas—and also that you have **enough time to have fun**, rest, and just **do little things that you like.**

But if you're **serious about pursuing your dreams**, and if you want to start building the life you want, then you need to take some time to *THINK LONG-TERM*.

Your long-term goal can be from *ANY AREA OF YOUR LIFE*. The long-term goal can be something like building a successful career in a specific field or making a difference on an issue you care about.

Don't panic if you still haven't decided on a long-term goal, because there are some activities we can do to help you get there.

Try this one right now.

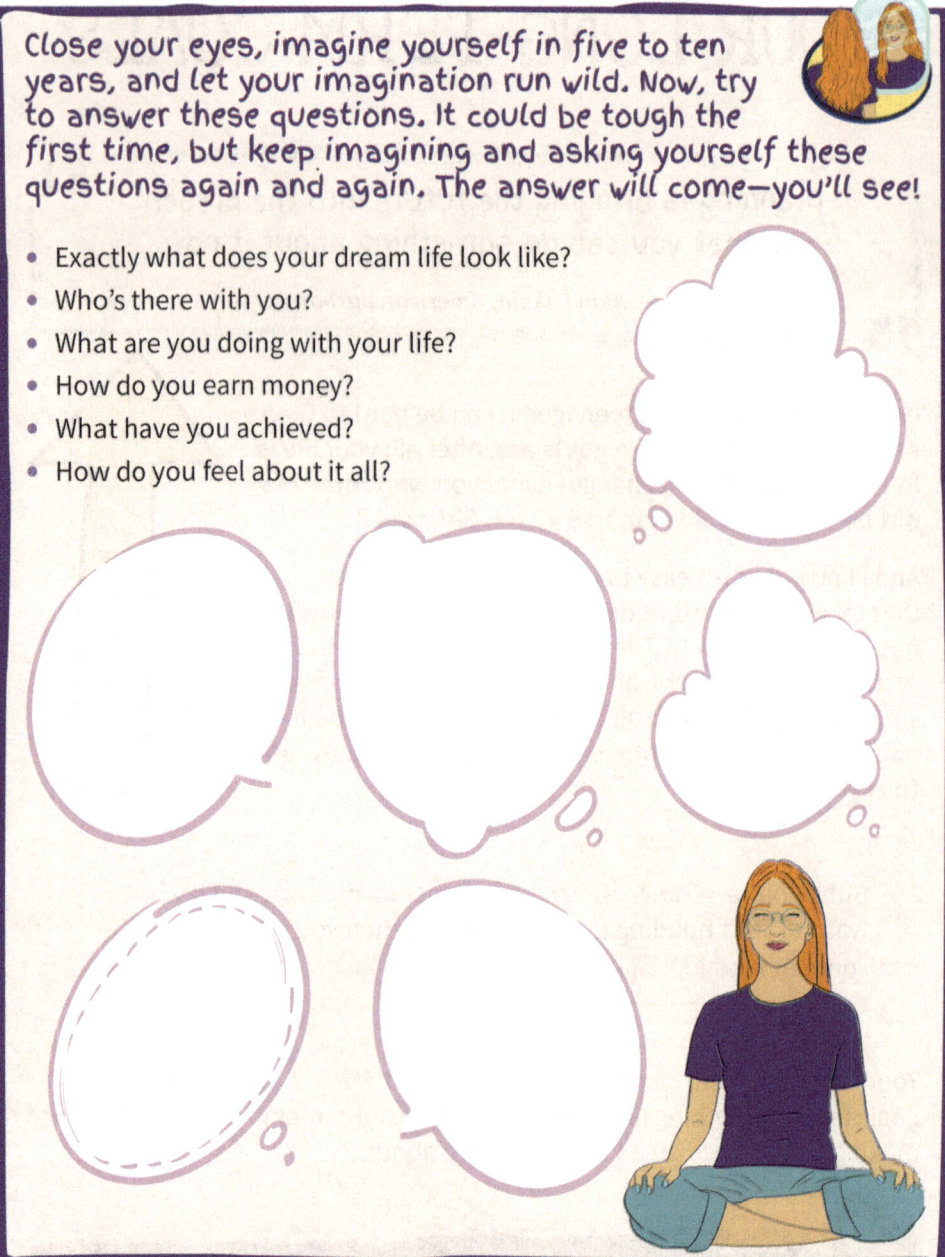

Close your eyes, imagine yourself in five to ten years, and let your imagination run wild. Now, try to answer these questions. It could be tough the first time, but keep imagining and asking yourself these questions again and again. The answer will come—you'll see!

- Exactly what does your dream life look like?
- Who's there with you?
- What are you doing with your life?
- How do you earn money?
- What have you achieved?
- How do you feel about it all?

THINK BIG! DARE TO WANT WHATEVER IT IS THAT YOU DREAM!

When you can see the big picture,
it's easier to stay focused on your goals.

> ## "THE GREATEST DANGER FOR MOST OF US IS NOT THAT OUR AIM IS TOO HIGH AND WE MISS IT, BUT THAT IT IS TOO LOW AND WE REACH IT.
>
> *— Michelangelo, Italian sculptor, painter, architect, and poet*

Need some inspiration? Here are a few examples of long-term goals that girls like you dared to set for themselves:

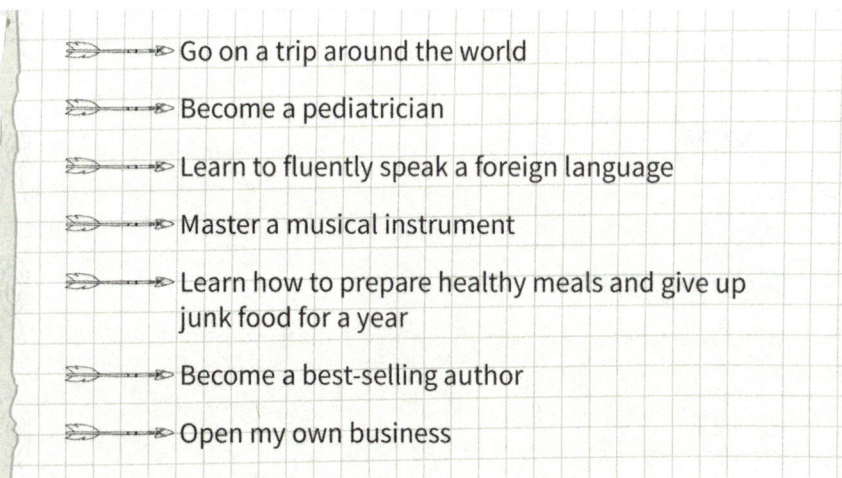

- Go on a trip around the world
- Become a pediatrician
- Learn to fluently speak a foreign language
- Master a musical instrument
- Learn how to prepare healthy meals and give up junk food for a year
- Become a best-selling author
- Open my own business

Life is about **BALANCE,** and most of us will have **more than one dream in life**—and there will probably be MORE THAN ONE GOAL. That's important because balance is a vital part of living a fulfilling life. And actually, that can help you to decide on your long-term goal too.

Take a look at this list that covers some of the main areas in life. And while looking at it, ask yourself these questions:

What do I want to accomplish in each
of the areas in the long term?

➤——➤ **MY HEALTH/FITNESS**

_____

➤——➤ **FAMILY LIFE**

_____

➤——➤ **SOCIAL LIFE**

_____

➤——➤ **CAREER**

_____

➤——➤ **EDUCATION**

_____

➤——➤ **MONEY AND FINANCE**

_____

➤——➤ **HOBBIES**

_____

➤——➤ **OTHER**

_____

Now mark the three goals that are the most important
goals for you—the ones you most want to achieve, the
ones you dream of most. These goals are the perfect
place to start.

Now, let's do more imagining. Girl, this is one of my favorite things to do, and it's easily the best part of the process. Choose **ONE** of the goals you picked in the previous exercise. Close your eyes and take a deep breath.

IMAGINE WHERE YOU WANT TO BE IN A YEAR, OR FIVE YEARS, OR MORE.

Ready, set, imagine!

In 1 year, I want to _____

In 3 years, I want to _____

In 10 years, I want to _____

In 20 years, I want to _____

Use these images and thoughts to help **shape your plans**.

Remember, my dear friend …

A GIRL WITH A PLAN IS A GIRL NOT TO BE UNDERESTIMATED.

AND GIRLS WITH PLANS TEND TO GET TO WHERE THEY'RE GOING.

Use the exercise above whenever you're making plans for the future or even when you're facing a challenge.

Think of it like a ROADMAP. You're on your way to see the latest chart-topping band, but you don't know how to get there. You grab a map, or you follow your sat nav, and voila, you get there in time for the gig.

Setting long-term goals can feel kind of strange at your age, I know. It's **hard to imagine** how and what you want to be in what feels like a million years from now. And sure, there's a big chance that **your long-term goal will change**, maybe more than once. And you know what? That's OK!

What matters is that you keep developing—always learning and striving to succeed in everything you do.

LIFE IS FULL OF CHALLENGES, AND EVERY EXPERIENCE IS A LESSON!

What are the things that you feel you're very good at?

NO ONE CAN TAKE YOUR KNOWLEDGE OR SKILLS FROM YOU.

How are you doing? Are you giving it your all? Are you making time for fun and hanging out too?

Every experience is a lesson, and each step forward helps take you toward what it is that you're meant to achieve. After all, if you eventually learn that **you don't want** something, **that's progress too!** And the same skills and knowledge can bring you success in more than one area.

I've had to change my goals several times. Did it happen to you too, Girl? Did you choose to do something but after a while you realized that it's not the right thing for you?

What did you choose to do?

What did you learn from this experience?

As Norman Vincent Peale said,

"Shoot for the moon. Even if you miss, you'll land among the stars."

It means that we are **more likely to achieve great things if we set our sights high.** The bigger our goal, the harder we have to work, and the more likely it is that we will achieve big things. If we don't achieve the big, big goal, we can still make our lives great. **The higher we aim, the more we can achieve,** even if it's not the original goal that we set out to accomplish.

PART 4

YOUR SHORT-TERM GOALS

> ❝ What you get by achieving your goals is not as important as what you become by achieving your goals. ❞
>
> — *Henry David Thoreau, American poet and philosopher*

Now that you have a long-term goal, it's time to set up your **short-term goals!**

There are two types of short-term goals:

1. SUPPORTED GOALS

Short-term goals that form **part of a bigger goal** are what we call "supported" goals because they support the larger end goal that you are working toward.

In the previous chapter, you tried to imagine what your life would look like in 1, 5, 10, or more years, and it's important to have that in your mind as we work through the next few activities.

> The first type of short-term goal is a BREAKDOWN of the long-term goal you set for yourself. These short-term goals are what will help you TO ACHIEVE your future goal and your dream. They SUPPORT the long-term goal that you have set.

For example, if your long-term goal is to open your own business at the age of 23, then your **supported short-term** goals would be:

- Learn basic accounting and financial management.
- Learn marketing and advertising.
- Study customer service.
- Learn about a business that succeeded and how they did it, or look at an unsuccessful business and figure out what to avoid.
- And more …

Let's try another little exercise.

Your long-term goal is to be a scientist,
or travel around the world, or become a chef.
What should your short-term goals be?

Let's choose one of the goals above and start practicing.

The **long-term goal** I chose to practice on is …

_____

Now, what are the **short-terms goals** that will help you achieve this long-term goal?

_____

_____

_____

_____

Now, choose one of **your own goals**!

My **long-term goal** is …

 _____

Now, what are the **short-terms goals** that will help you achieve this long-term goal?

 _____

_____

_____

_____

GOOD JOB, GIRL!

2. INDEPENDENT GOALS

Independent short-term goals are goals that are not necessarily part of a bigger, long-term dream. These goals are **goals on their own**, without having to be part of a bigger picture.

Not all your short-term goals are going to be part of a bigger plan, and sometimes you set a short-term goal **because it's something you want to do**. It doesn't always have to be part of the big plan.

For example, I have a few SHORT-TERM GOALS I dared myself to achieve during the last several years:

I dared myself to eat healthy food, at least five days a week.

I dared myself to develop an app by myself.

I dared myself to improve my grades in math (although it's not my strong area).

I dared myself to pass my driving test.

I dared myself to learn how to play chess.

I dared myself to read one book every week.

Now, what about you?

How do you want to dare yourself with an independent short-term goal?

Here are a few ideas—let's try it!

A challenge you want to master and never thought you could …

Something you are curious about …

Something that is fun or makes you feel better …

Something that is necessary or worth doing (yes, not all goals are things we choose or want to do …)

Something that will make you a better person …

Something you want to be perceived as …

A small, silly dream you have …

> **UNLESS COMMITMENT IS MADE, THERE ARE ONLY PROMISES AND HOPES; BUT NO PLANS.**
>
> — *Peter F. Drucker, management consultant and educator*

LET'S PRACTICE IT

We now know how to break down goals to help you move forward. Next, it's time to summarize your goals and make them much clearer and sharper.

> Remember, SETTING GOALS IS A SKILL—a skill that you can always improve on and get better at. The more you practice at this, the better you'll become.

Take a look at your LONG-TERM GOALS and your SHORT-TERM GOALS again.

Choose one of the long-term goals you thought of on page 18. It can be related to health/fitness, family, money, social life, education, or future career. Just choose whichever one you're most drawn to.

For now, just choose ONE long-term goal and write it down like a pro. And don't forget to implement all the tips and secrets we learned.

My long-term goal is ...

_____

My short-term goals (supported goals) are

#1 _____

#2 _____

#3 _____

Do you also have short-term independent goals? Of course you do, Girl!
List them here:

_____

_____

_____

_____

_____

PART 5

10 SECRETS TO HELP YOU PLAN LIKE A PRO

> ❝
> Rowing harder doesn't help if the boat is headed in the wrong direction.
>
> — *Kenichi Ohmae, Japanese author*

If you have a DREAM, Girl, you should turn it into a GOAL. **And when you have a goal, you need to have a PLAN to achieve it.**

That's because **dreams can come true if you have a plan**, and if you know how to plan like a PRO, you can **achieve them much quicker**!

And you can do it, Girl!

You can make a brilliant and powerful plan that could actually take you to the next level in your life.

Don't worry, Girl. You'll have everything you need! Just make sure to follow these SUPER-IMPORTANT RULES and HELPFUL TIPS, and they will help you BUILD YOUR POWERFUL PLAN!

> Remember, some things may work better for you than others.
>
> Some may work better for your **specific goal** and less for other goals.

Try the rules and tips **in the next pages** and see what works for you. **Ready, girl?**

1. WRITE IT DOWN

Did you know that people who **write down their goals** are three **times more likely to achieve them**? Yeah, it's that important. If your goal is important to you, make sure that you write it down. Make sure to capture all your goals electronically or in your special "I DARE MYSELF" notebook, and be sure to use the "MAKE-IT-HAPPEN" tool to write your plan too.

Your place to keep track of your goals, research, and new things you learn.

2. FIND SOMEONE WHO'S BEEN THERE BEFORE

For every goal, there are usually a number of people who've done it before, and sometimes they can be a really **good source of inspiration and information**. Depending on what your goal is, there are a number of ways you can benefit from talking to someone who's already achieved it.

Here are some questions to help you find them:

Do I know anyone who has **already** achieved my goal?	Where can I find them? Online? In my family? In the community?	What questions do I have about how they got there?	Is there any help I want to ask them for?

These people will often be ready to help, and they can offer advice on exactly how they got to where you want to be.

3. SET REALISTIC GOALS

We're all about creating big, bold, and ambitious goals, but it's also important to be realistic. There are certain goals that take time to achieve, and while most goals are possible for all of us, the key is to balance everything.

How do you know that your goals are realistic? Well, there is no recipe for that. It will come with experience. By **listening to your heart**. By **trying again and again**. You can start with SMALL goals and see how it goes. You can start with BIG goals and notice how that feels to you. It will become easier with time. Just keep practicing, and DON'T GIVE UP! You can do it! You're amazing! Don't forget that for a second!

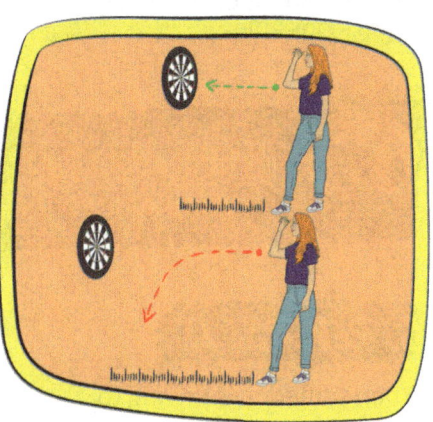

4. BE CLEAR, SHARP, AND SPECIFIC

It's also important to be super specific and get clear on exactly what it is that you want. The more specific you are when setting your goals, the more likely you are to achieve them.

Think of it like this—when you go into a restaurant, how do you order what you want? You ask for it, right? And you ask for EXACTLY what it is you want. You don't just say you want something tasty and warm. You tell them you want a certain kind of soup with a brown roll on the side. **Be specific with what you want, Girl!** It's the surest way of getting it.

5. GET CONTROL (AS MUCH AS POSSIBLE)

If you focus more on what YOU can do and less on what you DEPEND ON OTHERS to do, it will make it a lot easier to pursue your dream. If it's not something you have direct control over, then it's going to be harder to achieve. And you're going to want to give yourself the best chance possible.

 **Think about what you want and ask yourself this simple question—do I have control over this?**

6. REVERSE IT

When someone is driving to a place they've never been to before, they start with the end destination. Then, using a map, they work backward and identify the exact route they need to take to get there. What exit do they need to get off at? Which road will get them there the quickest? Starting with an endpoint is essential for any journey, and ultimately, that's what goals are, right?

Think of reaching your goals as being a bit like a map.

WHERE ARE YOU RIGHT NOW? WHERE ARE YOU GOING?

And what are the rough steps (short-term goals) you need to take in order to get to the end result you want?

7. BREAK IT DOWN (AND AGAIN, IF NEEDED)

Once you've decided on the short-term goals that are needed for each long-term goal, make sure that you **break them down again**. This time make them into small **TO-DO's**. The smaller the task, the **easier** it's going to be, and the more **motivated** you're going to be to reach your end goal.

It will also help you build momentum because the more actions we take, the easier it is to move forward. Breaking your short-term goals into smaller steps helps the entire process by ensuring that each completed task moves you on to the next one.

8. MAKE YOUR TIMELINE AN ESSENTIAL PARTNER

When we set ourselves a goal, it's important to make sure we have a **timeline for that goal**, because knowing when you want it done will **HELP YOU TO GET THERE**.

We all tend to spend **as much time on a task as we can**, meaning that if a task has no deadline, we will spend as much time as we want on it. If a task has a deadline, **we'll probably do it close to the deadline** and not before. Think about it for a second …

If your parent asks you to do something, how fast would you do it?

If they ask you to do it with a specific deadline, when do you usually do it—right away or close to the deadline? And what if there is no deadline …?

Setting a timeline will **keep you on track**, **motivate** you, and make sure you're **moving forward** toward your success.

Make sure to include a timeline in your plan. It's another essential part of getting to where you want to go.

9. GIVE YOURSELF CHECK-UP POINTS AND FOLLOW-UPS

One of the best tips I learned very early in my journey was to set check-ups and continually check in on my progress.

Have a routine for keeping up with your goals, and **follow it on a regular basis**. Every week, two weeks, or every month—see what works best for you, Girl—but sit down and check in on your goals. Look at your plan and where you're going—and how much further you have to go to get there.

Find **A FUN WAY** to track your goal because that's going to help you keep going. How about creating a **tracker with boxes** that you can mark for each step of your goal? What about a new **planner** that you could use to track your progress? Whatever it is, find something that helps **make the process fun**.

10. DON'T HIDE IT—PLACE YOUR PLAN IN FRONT OF YOU AND THE WHOLE WORLD

We all have many papers here and there. We all have lots of documents on our electronic devices. Make sure your plan is NOT just another piece of paper or one more file on your device.

You worked hard to have a wise and powerful plan. **Don't hide it**. Place it right there where you see it all the time. It's your dream in there. It's **your commitment to yourself**. It's your roadmap and recipe for success.

If you want to keep it to yourself, place it near your bed. If you want to share it with the world, place it in another central place in your house.

This plan is your declaration. Your statement. Place it where it is most visible as a reminder of your dreams and how you can achieve them!

On page 77 I created a checklist for you of all the tips mentioned here. When your plan is ready, use the checklist to make sure everything you need is included in your plan!

Part 6

YOUR RESOURCES-THE ESSENTIAL INGREDIENTS FOR SUCCESS

> "
> Success is a ladder that cannot be climbed with your hands in your pocket.
>
> — *Mark Caine, British analyst and strategist*

RESOURCES ARE KEY! THEY ARE SUPER, SUPER IMPORTANT.

 **You can have the best-written plan ever, and your motivation can be outstanding, but without the right resources, you won't get very far.**

OK, so what exactly are resources?

Resources are **the tools that help you get from A to Z**. I like to think of my resources as being **my toolkit**. They are the products and services that help me achieve my goals. The resources you will need are going to be different depending on what it is that you want.

Imagine that your goal is to become **a chef**, but that you don't have a **kitchen to cook in, equipment to cook with, or any way to learn how to be a chef**. Obviously, you lack a lot of resources—and you need to find ways around that problem.

Or maybe you want to be **a professional basketball player**, but you don't have **sports shoes or a team to join**. Again, you are lacking in resources.

On your path to success, you're going to need a lot of RESOURCES. Different resources will be important for different times and different goals, but

LEARNING TO IDENTIFY THEM AND FIND THEM IS KEY.

> A resource can be anything from materials to tools, time, money, or even other people—ANYTHING and EVERYTHING that can support you in reaching your goals. It could also be a book, an app, a website, or anything else that can help you reach your goals.

RESOURCES aren't just the physical tools you need to get to where you are going—they can also help you gain the **KNOWLEDGE** and **EXPERIENCE** you need to reach your goal.

> There are plenty of RESOURCES in the world. And the good news is **lots of them are FREE**, and many are AVAILABLE whenever you need them! You just need to choose wisely.

A key tip for success is to develop a WIDE COLLECTION OF RESOURCES. Or as I like to think of it, a toolkit of resources.

This is important because resources aren't usually "one-size-fits-all"—which means the same resource won't work in every situation. And they certainly won't all work for everyone. You may need **different resources to help you reach different goals** in different situations.

Anything worth doing is worth doing well.

Give it 100%!

Here are some of the resources you may need at some point or another:

ONLINE RESEARCH – Name any subject in the world, and you'll find dozens of photos, articles, blogs, vlogs, and other helpful videos to inform and inspire you. Not to mention the thousands of articles and eBooks that are also available online. There's so much information out there, and you just have to look for it.

BOOKS, MAGAZINES, AND OTHER MEDIA – For so many reasons, the library is a great place to spend an afternoon, and for us girl-go-getters, it is a huge resource. You can find up-to-date information and be inspired by the history and knowledge around you. Books, magazines, and newspapers cover just about every subject in the world.

SOFTWARE AND APPS – Software or mobile apps can be helpful in a lot of ways. They go way beyond just helping you learn new things. They can give you all sorts of important tools like timers, trackers, calendars, calculators, logs—whatever! There are apps for literally everything. There are even apps to help you be calm, take a deep breath, and focus on your goal.

MENTORS – A mentor is someone who influences you, someone who can guide you and give you direction as you are setting and achieving your goals. A mentor is someone you trust, someone who'll give you honest advice, and someone who's always rooting for you (just like me!). If you haven't already figured it out, a mentor can play a pretty important role in helping you achieve your goals.

Is there anyone you can think of who might be an awesome mentor for you?

_____

ADVICE AND FEEDBACK – It's not only mentors who can help—there are other people who may be able to give you some good pointers too. Sometimes people don't have the time to be a mentor, but they're still available for guidance and advice. Don't be shy! Seek people out and ask questions. Ask for feedback! Use it to learn and grow!

Oh, yes! Let's face it, Girl! Getting feedback can sometimes feel a little embarrassing or even insulting. It can be tough to admit there may be room for improvement. But there always is. The sooner you accept that fact, the sooner you can put the good feedback to work!

If it's tough to get advice or feedback in a certain area, chances are this may be the area where you need that advice and feedback THE MOST.

 **CIRCLES OF SUPPORT** – If you want to succeed, it's a good idea to surround yourself with friends and others who force you to level up. Find people who have a desire to learn and grow, just like you!

- Surround yourself with people who will **LEARN AND GROW TOGETHER with you** and share in your journey to success!

- **STAY AWAY FROM NEGATIVE PEOPLE!** Don't waste your time on people who tell you that it's not worth trying, or it's best to just give up.

- Seek out **POSITIVE PEOPLE** for support, advice, and feedback. I promise you—they are out there!

- Make friends who make you **A BETTER PERSON**.

 **OTHER MATERIALS** – There are, of course, a huge array of other materials out there, and the kind of resources that you need will probably be very personal, according to your goal.

If your goal has some kind of physical component, **you will probably need to borrow or buy it. It's worth doing your research on this before you start to invest.** After all, there's no point in purchasing professional pots and pans that you won't need until you've been a chef for 10 years. Instead, start with the basics. Create a list of the main products that you need.

Have a think: Who's the first person you would turn to if you needed a boost?

_____

Now that we understand what resources are and what role they can play in our goals, let's put that knowledge into practice. Here are a few goals that some of my friends have set for themselves. Can you help them work out what resources they are going to need?

Let's start with Beth. She wants to be **a runner.** She wants to enter **races and train every day**. So, what resources would she need to make that happen?

_____

_____

_____

_____

_____

What about Anna? She wants to learn **a foreign language**—or three actually, but she's focusing on one for now—what resources does she need?

Nǐ hǎo

Bonjour

Yassas

Hola

Shalom

_____

_____

_____

_____

_____

Finally, there's Alex, and she wants to design this **super cool app** that she's come up with. She's had the idea for a few months and has planned it all out, and she's ready to create it. What resources would help her get there?

_____

_____

_____

_____

_____

Resources have lots of different purposes, and there are plenty of them, which means there are resources to help with everyone's goals. They can be used to support you in so many ways!

Now let's focus on **YOUR OWN LIST OF RESOURCES**. Think about your goals and what resources you're going to need.

My Goal: _____

Resources needed:

☐ _____

☐ _____

☐ _____

☐ _____

☐ _____

Part 7

PLANNING WITH THE MAKE-IT-HAPPEN TOOL

> A good goal is like a strenuous exercise— it makes you stretch.
>
> — *Mary Kay Ash, American businesswoman*

By this point, you should have some idea of what you want for your future—the kind of goals you want to achieve, both big and small!

Now, it's time to take it to the next level.

It's time to stop planning on the fly and start planning LIKE A PRO with the MAKE-IT-HAPPEN tool!

We know that making a plan is an important skill to develop. But **you don't have to do it all on your own** because there are tools out there you can use to help you on your way.

One of the awesome tools I use for making plans is the

"MAKE-IT-HAPPEN" TOOL.

If you've read my first book, *You Can Be Whatever You Want, Girl!*, then you have already met this tool. But now, after the deep dive in this book, you can learn to use it **like a pro** and build a more powerful plan—one that will take you to the next level in your life.

Now is the time to dig down, practice more, and start planning like a real expert. **Don't worry. It's a process.** And **we'll go through it together.** I'm here to help, Girl!

MAKE-IT-HAPPEN EXPERT

THE MAKE-IT-HAPPEN TOOL

If you've not used it before, you're going to LOVE this process, and I am really excited to show it to you.

Take a look at **the MAKE-IT-HAPPEN** tool and what it includes:

* On pages 78-81 you can find two plain templates that you can practice on and use for your plans.

WHY IT'S BETTER TO USE THE MAKE-IT-HAPPEN TOOL

1. WRITING IT DOWN WORKS BEST.

When you write your thoughts and goals down on paper, you're already halfway to **putting them into action**. It makes you **more committed** and more likely to achieve your goals.

2. BLANK PAGES MAKE EVERYTHING FEEL HARDER.

We've all been there, right? You sit down to start your essay for school, and bam, the white page is there in front of you. And try as you might, nothing comes to you. It stays blank, and you stare at it, unsure of where to start.

YOU CAN AVOID THE BLANK PAGE IF YOU USE THE MAKE-IT-HAPPEN TOOL TO PLAN.

- **The page is already laid out for you, and your job is to just fill it in.**
- **It asks all the right questions. And asking good questions gets good answers.**

When you write things down on a well-organized planner, you have **a recipe for success**!

3. IT HELPS YOU MAKE IT HAPPEN.

The Make-It-Happen tool **includes everything you need to create and craft your powerful plan.** And as we know, once you have a plan, you can then start chasing your dreams.

> It's kind of like a recipe. Take the time, give it the right thought, fill it in completely, and you'll have the exact blueprint you need to start achieving your goal.

4. IT'S FLEXIBLE AND ADJUSTABLE—TO WORK FOR YOU.

The Make-It-Happen tool allows you to write your plan in the level of detail that you prefer. It gives you a framework, but **it's flexible enough to let you plan the way that works best for you**.

HOW TO WORK WITH THE MAKE-IT-HAPPEN TOOL

The Make-It-Happen tool includes **FIVE SIMPLE** but sophisticated and **challenging questions** that make you **think about the most important aspects of your plan.** And it's all organized in one document.

It might seem strange in the beginning, and maybe it won't be easy, but don't worry, Girl. **It will go smoother the more you practice and do it.**

Now, let's take some time to go through the tool and each one of the questions in it.

Let's imagine that you wish to bake a wonderful and special cream layer cake.

Your **goal** is to make this special **cake.**

But there is no ready recipe for it. You need to create your own recipe and bake it.

> The Make-It-Happen tool helps you create your own recipe for success.

Now let's start creating the recipe that will help you reach your goal!

STEP #1 – YOUR LONG-TERM GOAL

WHAT is the cake that you wish to bake? Can you get clear on it? What will it look like? When is it done? What will it taste like?

When it comes to making a plan, the first step is to **KNOW WHAT YOU WANT!** And then announce—loud and clear—exactly **WHAT YOUR LONG-TERM GOAL IS.** Make sure you write it down. But also say it out loud. It's your dream! Your goal! The thing you want to achieve and accomplish. It's what you're going to be focusing on and where you will direct your time and energy from now on. Because, Girl, **I know that you're committed to this**. After all, it's YOUR DREAM!

Write it with full meaning, as a promise, mostly to yourself, but you can also **share it with everyone** you want (especially those who can help you achieve it).

It's kind of like a declaration.
It's your vision of how you see yourself in the future.

One of my goals, which I also shared in my first book, You Can Be Whatever You Want, Girl!*, was to become **an author***. *So, using the **Make-It-Happen tool,** I wrote my goal like this:*

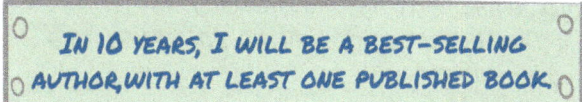

IN 10 YEARS, I WILL BE A BEST-SELLING AUTHOR, WITH AT LEAST ONE PUBLISHED BOOK.

*I also said it out loud, and I shared it with a few of my best friends—people who would support me on this journey. I even **prepared a little sign** and hung it near my bed. **It reminded me of what my goal was**, especially when I felt frustrated or too busy with other things (things that distracted me from working toward that goal). But then I would see the sign, and I would remember my goal again and exactly what I was working toward.*

Take a second to list one or two of YOUR long-term goals here:

In _____ years I will _____

In _____ years I will _____

MY LONG-TERM GOAL

Now say them loud and clear. Don't be shy at all! It might feel strange at first, but the moment you say it, your intentions become more real Go, Girl!

Sometimes it helps to imagine what your life will look like when you reach your goal … It can help you to be more accurate and also more motivated.

Here is what **I imagined** when I set my LONG-TERM GOAL to be an author:

When I'm an author, I will wake up every day and drink my coffee in my beach house (which I bought from royalties I earned). I will place my desk in front of the sea view and write my next book. I will listen to the sounds of the waves while writing and smelling the fresh air. I will devote a few hours every day to answering fans and readers who write to me.

From time to time, I will travel to an interesting place around the world to meet readers and to sign my book.

NOW YOU TRY, GIRL.

Close your eyes and imagine how your life will look and feel AFTER you reach your long-term goals.

Let's capture it!

When I reach my long-term goals, I'll be _____

I will _____

_____

_____

_____

_____

_____

OK! NOW WE HAVE THE VISION!
TIME TO MOVE ON TO THE NEXT LEVEL OF DETAILS.

STEP #2 – YOUR SHORT-TERM GOALS

What kind of layers do you need to create your special cake? How will every layer look and taste?

If you don't have the knowledge, skills, and experience in baking layer cakes, you can't just step into the kitchen and build a beautiful, tasty layer cake, can you?

Of course not. You need to start with the basics. You need to understand, learn, and practice **STEP-BY-STEP**, repeatedly.

So, the next step in achieving your long-term goals is to **BREAK DOWN** your big dream into **small, achievable short-term goals**. These short-term goals are the **ingredients and layers** that gradually make your big, beautiful cake. Each one will help you step a little closer to your final long-term goals.

So, what do you need to put into your cake's recipe? What small steps lead to your big goal?

☐ Everything you NEED TO LEARN

☐ Everything that you NEED TO DO

☐ Everything you NEED TO ACHIEVE

☐ All the things that can help you achieve this big dream

Remember the tip from earlier about "reverse engineering" your goals in order to understand the exact steps that you need to reach them. **It can also help if you write them in chronological order.** In essence, what smaller items do you need to include within each step of the process?

For my long-term goal, there are TWO specific short-term goals that run parallel to each other, meaning that I can work on these at the same time.

1. *Learn about the art and technique of good writing.*

2. *Learn about self-publishing.*

But the rest of my short-term goals are more in chronological order, and I plan to follow them step-by-step. These goals have to be done one after the other.

3. *Practice my own writing and editing and get feedback.*

4. *Publish my short story.*

5. *Write another new short story every six months.*

6. *Write my first full novel.*

A TIP—don't forget to revisit all the pointers I shared with you earlier before you start to list your short-term goals.

THE KEY IS TO MAKE SURE YOUR SHORT-TERM GOALS ARE SMALL AND ACHIEVABLE.

It's usually **better to have plenty** of short-term goals that you can achieve more quickly than to have **one general goal** that takes a lot of time to get done. That way you don't end up feeling overwhelmed and not able to move forward.

It's also hugely more fun—and encouraging—to **tick off as many short-term goals as you can while you move forward**. It's a lot more fun than being stuck with a big goal that takes lots of time and energy to accomplish. So don't get lazy.

Make **A LONG LIST** of short-term goals that you can reach in a relatively short period of time. That way, you can start enjoying your progress right away!

STEP #3 – TASKS

What do you need to DO to bake each layer of your cake? How are you going to go about it?

IT IS NOW TIME FOR ACTION! You know what your dream is (long-term goals), you broke it down into small, achievable short-term goals, and now what? What are you supposed to do about it?

Sure, you could start with action immediately and intuitively do things that can help you move forward. **But it's much better to have an organized, well-thought-out plan that you intend to follow.** This is where chronological order comes into play, as it makes it easier for you to follow through with your planned action.

As you can see, when it came to wanting to be a writer, my first short-term goal was to **learn about the art and technique of good writing**.

I had to make a plan for how to make that happen, and I made a list of the smaller tasks that I knew would help me to achieve it:

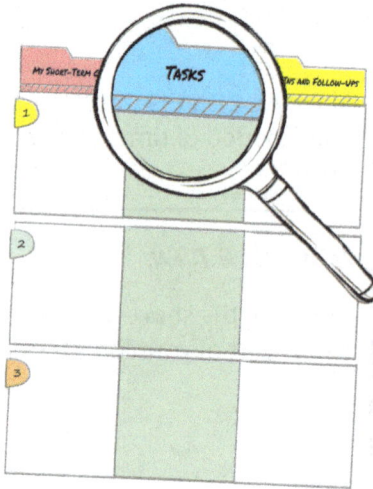

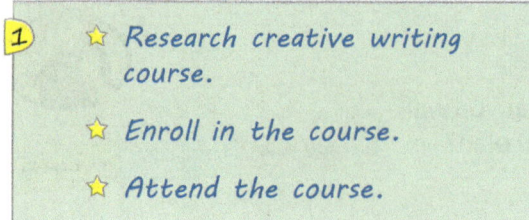

1
- ☆ Research creative writing course.
- ☆ Enroll in the course.
- ☆ Attend the course.

It might sound obvious, but it helps a lot, and it's so fun to check in and mark **DONE** next to each one of the tasks that I completed. It feels like progress. Like I'm on my way to success! Like I'm actually doing things to get to my dream!

So, you need to have a list of tasks for each one of your short-term goals!

Don't forget that your tasks must be simple and doable.

Try to create a list of tasks that **depend on you** and not on others. The more tasks you can do on your own, the more chance there is that you will accomplish them.

Also, don't forget to add a **timeline** to each task! It will motivate you. It will help you make sure you're moving forward, and it spells out your commitment to yourself!

Focus, Girl! Take a breather if you need to. Then refocus and crush it!

LET'S SEE YOU TRY IT NOW.

Choose one of your short-term goals
and break it down into tasks.

_____

_____

_____

_____

MY SHORT-TERM GOALS	TASKS	CHECK-INS AND FOLLOW-UPS
1	🔍	
2		
3		

Now, take a look at what you wrote.

Make sure your task is:

☐ Simple

☐ Doable

☐ Dependent on you as much as possible

☐ Timeline specific

STEP #4 – CHECK-INS AND FOLLOW-UPS

**How will you KNOW THAT your RECIPE
IS OK and you're on the right path to
making your dream layer cake?**

Now it's time to check in with your goals
on a regular basis, Girl, to **ensure that
you're on the right path** toward making
your dreams come true.

There are two options that can help
here. You can check for **yourself**, or
you can use a **check-in partner**. And of
course, you can also combine both.

Check yourself.

Checking yourself can be easy and fast, but it can also be a bit TRICKY …

If you want to do it right, you have to be very **honest with yourself**. This part of the plan means that you are the **judge** and the **inspector** of yourself and your own actions.

Yes! It's your dream. It's your plan. And if you want to achieve your goal, you sometimes need to **be strict with yourself**.

> **How often to check in?** Start by deciding how often to check-in. Weekly? Every other week? Monthly?

This will be different for every girl and for every goal. Mark check-ins in your calendar. It will help you remember that you need to **regularly look at your progress** and make sure you're going in the right direction.

Review it honestly.

Now here comes the tricky part … If you decide to review your goals every two weeks and you didn't make any progress in the last two weeks, it means that you still need to follow up and **update that there is NO PROGRESS**.

Remember, we have to be honest with ourselves. When you update that there's NO PROGRESS, you're not doing it just to be hard on yourself. It's because it helps you understand how **much time and effort it takes for you to do things** and that maybe you need to tweak things for next time. If there is no progress in your plan, maybe you need a little bit more time. Or maybe you need more help.

> **This is your private plan. You don't get any score or punishment if you don't do something. IT'S YOUR TOOL, Girl!**

We don't always do everything we plan, and **it's OK** to note it.

Use these three questions to help you stay on track:

1. AM I DOING WHAT IT TAKES TO COMPLETE MY SHORT-TERM GOALS?

2. AM I MOVING ALONG AT A GOOD PACE?

3. DO I NEED TO MAKE ADJUSTMENTS?

CELEBRATE YOUR PROGRESS.

And of course, **don't forget to CELEBRATE** when you complete tasks (or even do things ahead of time)!

Adopt a check-in partner.

One of the most effective ways to make sure you're on the right path is to find **a CHECK-IN PARTNER**. This could be a friend, a family member, a teacher, a coach—anyone who believes in you and wants to help you succeed.

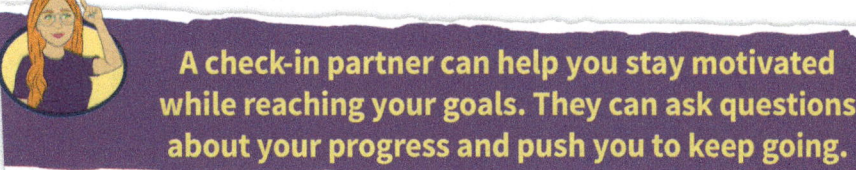

A check-in partner can help you stay motivated while reaching your goals. They can ask questions about your progress and push you to keep going.

A check-in partner doesn't have to have a lot of experience or knowledge about your specific goal. It can just be **someone who cares about you**.

Who's a good fit to be your check-in partner and help you follow up on your plan?

WHAT KIND OF CHECK-IN WOULD YOU LIKE TO HAVE?

CHECKING MYSELF / CHECK-IN PARTNER / COMBINATION

Why do you think this is the best way for you to follow up?

If you're not sure what would work best for you, Girl, that's OK. Here are three questions that might help you figure it out.

Mark the statement that is closest to what describes you best:

A. When you have a project to do for school, when do you usually do it?

1. At the very last moment, and sometimes I'm almost late …

2. I will finish it before the deadline, but I will recheck it and submit it just on time.

3. I will finish it ahead of time, immediately submit it to forget it, and go next to my other tasks.

B. How do you usually remember your tasks and manage them?

1. With the help of my parents or teacher. They remind me and check if I'm doing them on time.

2. I have a calendar, and I use a to-do list from time to time, but it also helps me to get support from others (parents/teachers/friends, etc.).

3. Everything is in my calendar or in my detailed to-do list. I always keep it up to date and make sure I'm on time with all my tasks.

C. Which sentence describes you the most?

1. Sometimes I feel overwhelmed with all the tasks and obligations I have in my life.

2. Most of the time, I feel good about managing my tasks and duties, but sometimes it's too much, and I feel I'm falling behind …

3. I'm almost always in control and manage my tasks with no special problems. I'm very organized and get good feedback about managing my time.

Great! Now, Give yourself one point for each 1. answer; two points for each 2. answer; and three points for each 3. answer. Then add up your points. Your total score should be a number between 3 to 9.

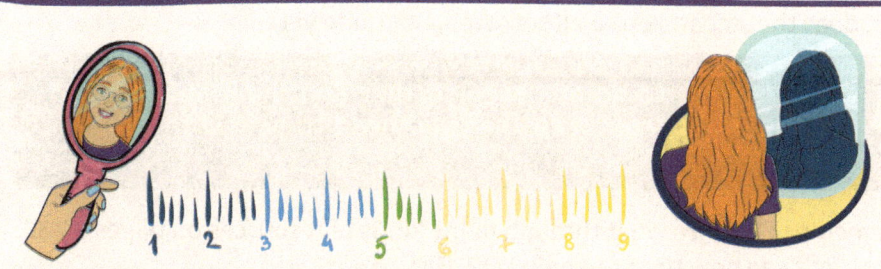

If your score is closer to **3 or 4 points**, it means that it's much better for you to **use a check-in partner**. Maybe you'll only need someone to help you with the check-in process in the beginning— to have a smooth start—and then you can move on with checking in by yourself. Or maybe keeping a check-in partner is the best way for you to succeed with your plan. You'll never know until you try it, Girl …

If you scored closer to **8 or 9 points**, it means that it's not a problem for you to follow up on your plan by yourself if you want to. You don't necessarily need someone to do this process with you—you'll do fine with self-check-ins.

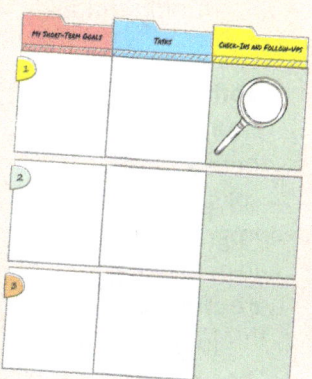

Of course, you can, and should, try both options! That way you can know what's the best way for you to follow up on the progress of your plan.

WHAT DO YOU NEED to make your dream cake? What ingredients do you need to have to make the cake you want?

You now have a detailed plan, Girl! And I'm sure you're ready to start working very hard on the plan you've created to achieve your dream.

So, does that mean you're all set? Well, not quite yet …

> Now it's time to go one step further and think about the essential resources that you need to help with your success.

Remember that we went through many kinds of resources on pages 34-36. Now let's see how they can help YOU, Girl.

Sometimes it can be difficult to identify your resources, but these questions can help you get there.

Online research – Are there any relevant websites, online courses, articles, or other online information that can help you?

Books, magazines, and other media – Are there any books, magazines, or other media that specialize in the topic you want to research or learn?

Software and apps – Are there any apps or software programs that can help you be more effective on this journey?

Mentors – Is there anyone who can help you in the area you chose?

Advice and feedback – Are there any people whose opinions you value or whose point of view, tips, or advice you think you can benefit from?

HELPFUL RESOURCES FOR ACHIEVING MY GOALS

Circles of support – Who are the people that you need to stand by your side while you're working hard on this journey to accomplish your goals?

Other materials – Are there any materials, tools, or products that are essential to doing your tasks and achieving your goals?

NOW YOU, GIRL! TRY TO MAKE AN INITIAL LIST OF THE ESSENTIAL RESOURCES YOU ARE GOING TO NEED.

HELPFUL RESOURCES FOR ACHIEVING MY GOALS

And the journey begins …

LET'S START PLANNING WITH THE MAKE-IT-HAPPEN TOOL

The big moment arrives, and you have everything you need to start planning with this awesome Make-It-Happen tool!

As you write your plan, remember it can be as detailed or as basic as you want or need it to be.

Depending on your goal, it can include just a few **steps**, or there may be many steps you need to do to achieve what you want.

It could be organized by **time** or by **topics**.

It could be super fun, **colorful**, **handwritten**, or **printed out**.

The only requirement is *THAT IT HELPS YOU!*

A good plan is a TOOL that helps YOU achieve **your dreams** and **goals**. So, it has to be what YOU need it to be. Your plan needs to be clear to you, supportive of you, and able to serve you in every way it can.

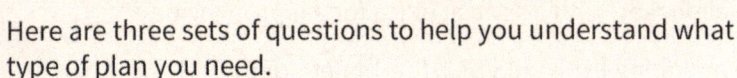

NOW, LET'S FIND OUT TOGETHER WHAT WORKS BEST FOR YOU, GIRL!

Here are three sets of questions to help you understand what type of plan you need.

Check the level of detail you prefer by marking the statement that's closest to what you usually feel.

A. When you make social plans with your friends, you check a few basic details like who will be there and generally what you're going to be doing.

B. When you make social plans with your friends, you check details like what time to meet, how long the get-together will last, who's going with whom, and what the planned activities are.

C. When you make social plans with your friends, you only need to know in general when and where to meet.

D. You usually prefer to have a detailed list of to-dos, with every single task written down, including all details needed.

E. Your to-do list is usually just a rough outline of what you need to get done. You don't need too many details.

F. Your to-do list is usually a mix of some specific, detailed items and some general items, depending on each task.

G. You prefer to get a more general and open assignment for homework. Too many details confuse you and don't allow you to express yourself the way you want.

H. You prefer your homework assignment to have some details to help you be more focused—but not too many.

I. You prefer your homework assignments to be as detailed as possible because it helps you to understand better and make sure they're done correctly.

J. Your shopping list would be very detailed and include alternatives, something like this:

- White T-shirt, size M loose, V-neck, no print, possibly a small pocket on the chest

- Black comfortable backpack with black zippers and at least one external pocket, with a special place for a laptop inside

K. Your typical shopping list would be a few bullet points with just a few details about what you were looking for:

- White T-shirt, size M, V-neck

- Black comfortable backpack

L. If you needed to prepare a shopping list, you'd jot a short note that generally described what you wanted:

- White T-shirt

- Comfortable backpack

Now, in the table below, circle only the letter of the answers you marked. Then, add up the points for each answer you circled.

Question No.	A	B	C	D	E	F		MY TOTAL
Scoring	2	3	1	3	1	2		POINTS:
Question No.	G	H	I	J	K	L		
Scoring	1	2	3	3	2	1		_____

What your score tells you about yourself:

4-6 points - You are a macro girl!

You're the queen of headlines. All you need is a general direction. You don't need too many details—just a general description and you're all set. In fact, too many details can confuse you or maybe block your creativity. So a plan with fewer details may work best for you.

A TIP – Check from time to time to see if adding a few more details could help you to better carry out your plan or follow up more easily. Sometimes the effort of adding more detailed steps can help. It's worth a try.

7-10 points - You are a mixed macro/micro girl!

You need some level of detail but not too much—just the general direction plus a few more details, and you're all set. You don't like to have too many details, but you need more than just a general description of your goals or tasks.

A TIP – Try to challenge yourself from time to time and check if more details could help you—or on the other hand, if eliminating some details would help more. Only experience will tell you which combination of details is best for you. So it's worth it to experiment.

11-12 points - You are a micro girl!

You're the queen of details. You like things spelled out in-depth, and you do well with lots of details. You love to have everything well planned and documented. It helps you feel prepared and in control!—and it makes follow-ups easier for you.

A TIP – Be careful about having too many details. You know what they say, "Sometimes you can't see the forest for the trees." That means if you have too many details, you can't see the whole picture (or your whole plan!). Check from time to time to see if less-detailed descriptions of your goals and tasks can help you to follow up more easily or even be more creative.

Part 8

WHAT HAPPENS WHEN YOU PLAN WELL AND YOU STILL CAN'T ACHIEVE YOUR GOALS?

> When it is obvious that the goals cannot be reached, don't adjust the goals, adjust the action steps.
>
> — Confucius, a Chinese philosopher

Wow, Girl! You're now much more **skilled with setting goals**, and you're starting to dare yourself with challenges and things that you want to achieve. It's exciting, but **will it be enough to ensure you succeed and achieve your dream?** Well, not exactly.

Dreaming out loud, setting your goals, and making your plan is the first BIG STEP. But what if you've followed all the steps for making **your PERSONAL POWER PLAN**, and it hasn't helped you move toward your goal? It's time to **evaluate the plan**.

SO, HOW CAN YOU KNOW IF YOUR PLAN IS RIGHT?

Well, there are many kinds of plans, Girl. And a good plan is one that **helps YOU achieve whatever YOU WANT**.

So, how will you know if you've written a good plan? It's simple! It's a good plan if **YOU USE IT** and it **helps you reach your goals**. If you said yes to either of these, then you wrote a good plan! **If you wrote a plan and you don't use it—it's probably not a good plan FOR YOU.**

When I wrote my first plan, I was very proud of it. I showed it to everyone, and they were all so impressed. I proudly hung it near my desk so I could see it.

==The problem was, I only looked at it a few more times after I put it up—and that was it.== It just stayed there as a nice piece of colorful décor. But I didn't use it at all. Unsurprisingly, I didn't make any major progress.

It took me some time to realize that I still wanted to stick to the same goal, but to do that, I had to change THE WAY I PLANNED IT. If I wanted it to work for me, ==I realized that it needed to be more detailed.== I needed to break it down into more short-term goals and step-by-step tasks so I had more small and achievable actions. Why? Because that's what works for me— that's how I like to get things done.

==I learned that a detailed plan helps me feel that I'm progressing== by ticking off small tasks along the way. And I also learned that doing it that way kept me connected to the written plan. I marked every task I completed and updated the next one, so the plan felt more active and more present in my life.

My next plan was much better, but it took a few goes for me to get it right. I had to make some major corrections, but eventually, I understood what the best plan for me was. ==Now, I'm much more skilled at writing plans.== It comes more naturally. I do it quickly and more often now. But I wasn't like that with the first plans that I wrote.

What is a good plan FOR YOU? I'm sure you'll find out soon! Just don't get frustrated too quickly. Take your time. Stick to it. You'll find your best way, I promise.

> " SUCCESS COMES FROM GOING FROM FAILURE TO FAILURE WITHOUT LOSS OF ENTHUSIASM. "
>
> — *Winston Churchill, former Prime Minister of the United Kingdom*

OK, so maybe you used the Make-It-Happen tool correctly and created the right amount of detail for you, but things still aren't going the way you planned. It happens to everybody, Girl! It has happened to me many times. And even **the most successful women in the world have failed many times before they've succeeded**.

> The key is **how you deal with this** and how you **LEARN from it** to move forward.

Here's what I do. When I face a major bump in the road, I stop **before** getting frustrated and giving up.

What does that mean? While it's very important to **REEVALUATE** your plan, you should **NOT ABANDON YOUR DREAM**.

Revisit your plan. You can make tweaks and adjustments. You can edit things and rehash them. That's not failing.

You only fail when you believe that you can't achieve what you've set out to achieve.

WHAT TO DO WHEN THINGS STILL AREN'T GOING THE WAY YOU PLANNED

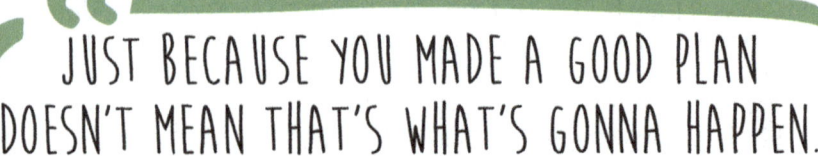

" JUST BECAUSE YOU MADE A GOOD PLAN DOESN'T MEAN THAT'S WHAT'S GONNA HAPPEN. "

— *Taylor Swift, American singer-songwriter*

There are several reasons why a **good plan can go wrong** and why you find yourself feeling stuck and frustrated.

If it happens to you (like it happens to me and many other girls), check the scenarios below. Then decide what you can change or how you can redo your plan so it will better help you achieve your goals.

Nothing in the plan works. Tasks are too hard to achieve, and I'm late on my deadline. It looks good on paper, but it simply doesn't work in real life!

Sometimes, when we sit in front of the paper, we tend to imagine that things are easier or quicker to do than they really are. Sure, Girl, if you only had to worry about one goal and it was the only thing you had to deal with, it would be easier. But **life is full of distractions** and new obligations, and your goals and tasks can become more challenging to get done than you expected.

What can you do about it?

- Make sure your goals are more realistic!
- Try breaking down every short-term goal into even smaller, more easily doable tasks.
- Give yourself more time.
- Get more help and support.

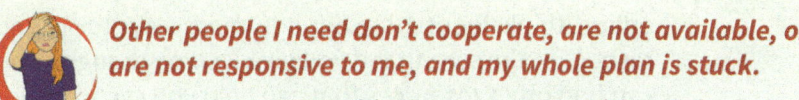

Other people I need don't cooperate, are not available, or are not responsive to me, and my whole plan is stuck.

Yes, there are many things **we can't do without the help of other people**. Every plan includes a few tasks that depend on others, who aren't always available—at least not in the way you want and in the timeframe that **you** needed them to help.

What can you do about it?

- Make sure your goals include as many tasks as possible that are **under your control** and not dependent on others. Try to find ways to do more by yourself, or if necessary, change your timeline. Sometimes it just means you need to think **more creatively**. You can do it, Girl! Be creative!

- Try to get the people you need more engaged in your plan. Show them your plan, ask for their feedback, check whether they can help and how much. **Let them**

know how much it means to you. When people—family members, teachers, friends, and others—**feel part of the plan**, they tend to **help more** and let you down less. Try it!

- Try to think of **more than one person** who can help. If you can, come up with a pool of people who might be able to help you. The more people and options you have, the less chances for your plan to get stuck.

- Make sure your plan includes **short-term goals and tasks to be carried out in parallel**. If you're stuck on one short-term goal or task, at least you can move on with another one.

I just don't have the resources to make my plan work.

Sometimes your goals and the way you break them into tasks are well planned, but you don't have the resources you need to achieve them.

What can you do about it?

- Well, time to be even more **creative**, Girl! Try to find **other alternatives**. Chat with more people, check online, think about more options, more ways to get your resources. I'm sure that if you give it some thought, you can find other resources that can help you carry out your plan.

- If you lack resources for one part of the plan, it doesn't matter. You're not completely stuck. Try to work on **ANOTHER PART OF THE PLAN**. Don't stop. Don't let it frustrate you. Maybe later, things will work better, and you'll get all the resources you need.

> "TO ACHIEVE GREAT THINGS, TWO THINGS ARE NEEDED: A PLAN AND NOT QUITE ENOUGH TIME."
>
> — *Leonard Bernstein, American composer and conductor*

I just don't have the time and energy to execute my brilliant plan now. Maybe later …

You have a great detailed plan, but somehow you just don't get to it. Oh, it has happened to me so often … Life is full of unexpected events and tasks. And as days pass by, you can't find time for the MUST-DO tasks, so how can you find time to dedicate to your long-term goal? Well, let me tell you what my grandmother says, Girl:

> It's never the right time to do what you want. So, START NOW. The sooner, the better.

What can you do about it?

- **Keep your goals in mind in every possible way**—write your goal on a big sign and hang it in your room, print out your Make-It-Happen plan and put it in a visible place … I bet you get the idea!

- Find a **check-in partner** and schedule a recurrent meeting to go over the plan, help you get motivated, and find more solutions.

- Make a deal with yourself—**treat yourself** every time you complete a task. Spoil yourself with something that makes you happy, something you usually don't do …

I know myself—I can't do it. I never have …

Girl, it is super important that you **let go of the past!** MAKE A FRESH START. You were younger, and you didn't have the knowledge and experience that you have now.

If you failed to achieve something in the past, it doesn't mean that you'll fail again!

Even if you face a big challenge now, you have new tools to help you. You have everything that you've learned in this book. You can make it better now and gradually succeed at what you want to do.

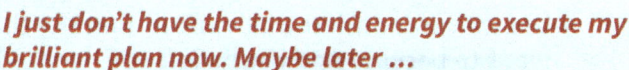

What can you do about it?

Have you ever heard of an **affirmation**? An affirmation is a **phrase**, **belief**, or **sentence** that we REPEAT OVER AND OVER AGAIN **until we believe that it is true**.

- **Use affirmations!** **You can affirm that the things you want to become and the beliefs** you need to have are already true. Instead of telling yourself that you can't do it, tell yourself that **YOU CAN**. Here are a few examples: Keep telling this to yourself.

"I can achieve any goal that I set my mind to."

"I can do things I've never done."

"I can be whatever I want."

- **Think POSITIVE!** Don't fill your mind with a negative thought that will prevent you from moving forward and achieving your dream.

  o Every bump in the road is a <u>challenge</u>—not a <u>failure</u>.
  o Every delay is an opportunity to learn and get better!
  o Instead of thinking, "**THIS IS TOO HARD,**" say to yourself, "**It takes more effort and time, but I can do it!**"
  o Instead of thinking, "**I GIVE UP,**" say to yourself, "**It's not as easy as I imagined, but I can figure it out and find a solution!**"
  o Instead of thinking, "**I ALWAYS MAKE MISTAKES,**" say to yourself, "**Of course I make mistakes. It's proof that I'm TRYING!**"

- **Engage more people who love you to support your plan and help you reach your dream.** They can encourage you and motivate you, and sometimes a little bit of love and support from our beloved people can do magic …

- Ask yourself **WHY YOU FEEL THIS WAY.** What is it that makes you think you can't achieve your goal? **Asking good questions gets good answers**, and it can help you understand the reasons behind your feeling that you can't do what you planned.

- **Ask yourself as if talking to a friend.** The next time you start telling yourself you can't do it, try flipping things around and thinking, **If this was a close friend of yours, what would you say to her instead?**

> ## "IT TAKES AS MUCH ENERGY TO WISH AS IT DOES TO PLAN."
>
> — *Eleanor Roosevelt, former First Lady of the United States*

Keep it up, Girl! Give it everything you can!

This whole plan makes me feel stressed and nervous, even shutdown …

We all **feel stressed** and a little nervous when we have a lot on our minds and need to take care of so many things in our lives: school, afterschool activities, family, friends, and more … Sometimes it's a little bit too much. I get it, Girl!

Sometimes you push too hard, and you are **overwhelmed** by all the tasks and goals you set. You can find yourself way too stressed and nervous. Sometimes it can shut you down, and you just can't go on.

If you feel too stressed and overwhelmed … If you feel this whole plan makes you a bad version of yourself rather than a better version of yourself, and it's starting to affect your life negatively … **It's time to recalculate your route.**

What can you do about it?

- Double-check your goals and tasks.
  - Maybe it's **too much at this stage**, and you need to break it into a smaller piece and give it a little more time.
  - Maybe you need to **adjust your short-term goals** so they're more realistic and doable.
  - Maybe you need more **help and support**.

- Sometimes you just need to let it go for a while and give yourself a little break. **Let it go for now. That's OK!** Do something else that makes you happy and relaxed. Then go back and revisit your plan.

Don't be afraid to adjust your plan. **It takes time to find the right load that you can carry** and the right tasks and resources that can move you forward.

Take a break. Then start again. **But don't let your dream go, Girl.**

DON'T GIVE UP! YOU CAN DO IT, GIRL!

Be **A GOAL ACHIEVER**, not only a goal setter. Don't just set your goals.

GO GET THEM, GIRL!

> " ONLY THOSE WHO DARE TO FAIL GREATLY CAN EVER ACHIEVE GREATLY. "
>
> — *Robert F. Kennedy, former United States Attorney General*

Try to remember an event in your life when you felt you didn't do well or you failed or gave up.

What was the occasion?

How did you feel?

What did you do about it?

What would you like to tell yourself, now that you are rethinking it?

Now, after learning more about how to deal with these situations, how have you handled things DIFFERENTLY?

Here is something else I want to remind you of about this incident—

IT WAS IN THE PAST. Now, FOCUS ON THE FUTURE, GIRL!

YOU ARE WISER NOW.

You have more tools to figure things out in your life. And you know much better how to deal with them.

So, don't be afraid to fail—it just means that **you are learning and trying**. Don't give up! Keep working on your goals!

P.S. In my book "You Can Be Whatever You Want, Girl!", you can find more about **how to LEARN FROM MISTAKES**. There is an awesome tool called **MAKE-IT-BETTER** that can help you learn from the past and be a much better version of yourself in the future.

Part 9

CELEBRATE YOUR PROGRESS AND ACHIEVEMENTS!

> The more you praise and celebrate your life, the more there is in life to celebrate.
>
> — Oprah Winfrey, American talk-show host, producer, actress, author, and philanthropist

If you set enough goals and create enough plans, eventually you are going to start ACHIEVING YOUR GOALS because that's what goal-getters do, Girl!

And when you do, it's super important that you take a moment to be **present and proud** of what you have done.

Every time you achieve a goal, and before you move on to the next one, you should take a moment to **celebrate how far YOU have come**. Don't wait until you reach your final goal. **Girl, you deserve to celebrate each and every step and achievement you accomplished!**

CELEBRATE BOTH SMALL AND BIG VICTORIES.

You are amazing! It's amazing that you are achieving what you want, and you should celebrate that at every opportunity.

Remember, Girl, celebrating your progress will keep you motivated and on the right track. Look back frequently throughout your journey and be **PROUD OF YOUR PROGRESS**.

What is the one thing you love to do most? Without even thinking, what is the one thing that feels like a celebration whenever you do it?

It's also possible to have more than one thing. Can you think of any other things you can do to celebrate your goals?

Now, let's create a list of ideas for how you're going to celebrate your progress and success. I call it a "Sweat Celebrations list."

I have a long **sweat celebrations list** I created during the years. My list includes my favorite ice cream, walking on the beach, listening to my favorite music, and coffee with a good friend—for the little accomplishments and victories. And, for significant progress and achievement, I've listed going to a good restaurant, a vacation in a place I choose, or a weekend getaway.

Now, Girl, let's start building YOUR **Sweat Celebrations list**.

How would you celebrate nice, small progress?

Small Progress Celebrations

How would you celebrate big progress and achievements?

Big Progress Celebrations

DON'T KEEP YOUR PROGRESS TO YOURSELF!

Your **family**, **friends**, and everybody around you who's part of your life, part of your **support circle—share it with them too!** Celebrate with them! Share how excited you are about it!

Use this opportunity to **express your gratitude and appreciation to them**. After all, they are your support circle, and you couldn't do it without their help or presence. Let them know what THEY mean to you.

Sharing your success (and your challenges!) with others usually helps them to **be more engaged in your goal**—and to have more empathy for you and the process you're going through.

Here's something that may sound a little strange to you, but if you do it, you'll feel the power of it!

Write a letter of APPRECIATION to yourself, for being amazing and doing your BEST.

You can write it on a nice, decorated sheet of paper and put it in an envelope, or you can write it in your I DARE MYSELF notebook. Write it. Then read it. It's all yours, and the power of the words will do the magic.

You can also add this activity to your Sweat Celebrations list.

Try your first one now. It can go something like this (or any style that works for you):

Dear _____ (write your name here),

I wanted to write to you to let you know that I see how much effort you put into achieving your goal to be _____. I see how much you _____ and also _____.

I know sometimes it's not easy, and you struggle with _____, but I'm sure in time, it will get easier and easier.

I know you are concerned about _____, but I believe in you! And I'm sure you'll learn how to figure it out.

I see how hard you work pushing toward your goals now _____ and how well you perform your tasks _____ and _____.

I'm proud of you! And I'm not the only one.

Keep going, Girl! You have people who love you and are there for you!

Part 10

LIRI'S TOP 10 TAKEAWAYS FOR YOU

You made it. You now know so much about setting goals, planning, and achieving them! Let's recap the top 10 takeaways.

1. IF YOU HAVE A DREAM— MAKE IT COME TRUE! IF YOU WANT SOMETHING—GET IT!

Dreaming about something and wanting it **will not Make It Happen, Girl**. If you want to achieve something, you need to take the steps that will make the dream a reality. That's where goals come into the picture.

You need to have a clear goal for what you wish to achieve! And then you **NEED TO PLAN WISELY.** Your plan is the map to your desired destination in your future life. It's your recipe for success.

2. SET YOUR LONG-TERM GOAL

If you're serious about pursuing your dreams, or if you want to build the life you want, then you need to take some time to **THINK LONG-TERM.**

Long-term goals can sometimes take years to achieve, but they're important because they **help you FOCUS YOUR ENERGY AND RESOURCES and ignore the day-to-day distractions.**

Your long-term goal can be from any area of your life. Think big! **Dare to want whatever it is that you dream!** And when you see the big picture, stay focused on your goals.

3. MAKE YOUR SHORT-TERM GOALS

Your short-term goals help you **make progress on your BIGGER GOALS**, keeping you on track. Short-term goals can usually be reached in a few days, weeks, or months.

Short-term goals help make your long-term goal feel that much more **achievable** because you'll be **slowly chipping away at it**.

They will also encourage you to keep going, because ticking them off will give you the **taste of success much more quickly**!

4. USE THE MAKE-IT-HAPPEN TOOL TO PLAN

Girl, when you write your goals and plans down on paper, you're already halfway toward achieving them. When you write them down on **a well-organized planner, you have a recipe for success**!

The Make-It-Happen worksheet includes everything you need to create the best possible goal-driven plan. Take the time needed to fill out all parts of the worksheet **properly and wisely**, and **make sure you use it**. If you do it right, it will become your recipe for achieving your goals and making your dreams come true! If not, try again. Sometimes, it takes more than one try. It takes time to practice and find the best way FOR YOU to write your plan so that it's easy to achieve your goals. Try again and again if needed. You'll get there. I promise!

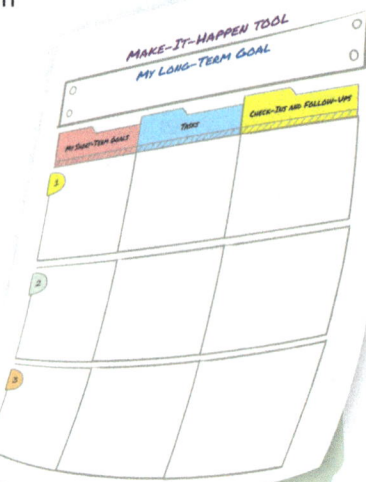

5. FIND THE BEST WAY FOR YOU TO PLAN

There are innumerable ways to create a plan for your goals, but finding what works for you is the only way to make it work.

The plan can be as **detailed** or as basic as you want or need it to be. It can include a few **steps** or many steps. It could be organized by **time** or **topics**, and it could be super fun, **colorful**, **handwritten**, or **printed out**.

It can be anything that **HELPS YOU** to drive yourself forward and achieve your dreams and goals.

6. SET REALISTIC AND SPECIFIC GOALS AND MAKE SURE THEY'RE IN YOUR CONTROL

You already know, Girl, that I'm all about thinking **big**, **brave**, **and bold**. But good goal setters ensure that their goals are also **realistic and specific**. Make sure your goals are realistic. If not, maybe you need to start with something a little bit more achievable. Then ask yourself if **your goal is clear enough**.

Remember, it's like ordering food in a restaurant. You ask for exactly what you want. You don't just broadly describe it. Same with goals—you need to be **very clear about what you want to achieve!**

And when you're planning out your goals, make sure that most of them are **within your control** and less dependent on help from others.

7. SET A TIMELINE

The timeline will help you be **more organized** and will also **motivate you** to **move forward**. Knowing when you want it done will help you get it done! A timeline will help direct your attention, **keep you focused**, and give you a deadline for what you want to have achieved.

So, **be sure to add a timeline and update it if necessary.** You can do it, Girl! You can control your time and the way you manage your days!

8. MAKE SURE YOU HAVE THE RIGHT RESOURCES

Resources are a HUGE key to your success. Your resources are your **TOOLS**, and you need good tools to achieve your goals. **A strong list of resources can help you achieve your goals more quickly** and smoothly and can be a support system for your plan.

Books, articles, apps, websites, libraries, newspapers, magazines, videos, role models, mentors—the list goes on and on. Because there are so many resources available to you, it shouldn't be too difficult to find the ones that work best for you. And **if one resource doesn't work for you, find another one.** It's there, Girl! All you need to do is find it.

9. SCHEDULE REGULAR CHECK-INS

Setting goals and meeting your plan's deadlines is not part of your school assignments or parents' requests. **IT'S ALL YOURS!** But that also means you need to find a way to **ensure you're moving forward** with your goals.

Scheduling a series of regular check-ins can help a lot here. It will **create momentum**, and this momentum will keep you **progressing**. Be sure to check in with **yourself** or with other **partners** to keep track of your progress regularly.

10. CELEBRATE YOUR PROGRESS AND ACHIEVEMENT

Don't wait until you reach your final goal, Girl. You deserve to celebrate each and every step and achievement you accomplish!

Celebrate both small and big victories.

You are amazing! It's amazing that you are achieving what you want, and **you should celebrate that at every opportunity.**

Your family, friends, and everybody around you who's part of your life, part of your support circle—**share it with them too!** Share how excited you are about it! Celebrate with them!

Celebrating your progress will keep you motivated and on the right track. Look back frequently throughout your journey and be PROUD OF YOUR PROGRESS.

Go, Girl! You're doing it. You're well on the way to achieving your goals and living your dreams!

Last but not least ...

My dear friend,

I am so proud of you. You have done it, and you are now ready to start taking actions that will lead you to the next level of your life. You should be proud of yourself, Girl!

Remind yourself,

"I HAVE A GOAL, AND I AM COMMITTED TO ACHIEVING IT!"

Determine what it is that you truly want, be consistent, and remain true to yourself.

Don't be afraid to go out of your comfort zone—be daring, be brave, and take risks.

And don't be afraid to ASK FOR HELP—because that's something else all successful people have to do at some point or another.

At the beginning of this book, I told you how excited I was for you to start planning your goals and pursuing your dreams! And now I'm excited to see you're actually doing it!

One last thing before you go and take over the world ... I believe in you and I am always here for you! I promise that whenever you need me, I'll be here and all you have to do is open this book.

Lots of love,
Liri

P.S. You can meet me and others like you and get more tips and inspiration here:

 www.facebook.com/Liri.Inspires
 www.instagram.com/liriinspires

LIRIINSPIRES

BONUS CHECKLIST

Sometimes there's so much to remember and you're not sure if you did everything right. Don't worry! I've got you covered with a short checklist of **all the steps you need for your powerful plan**.

 ☐ Write it down!

 ☐ Find someone who's been there before.

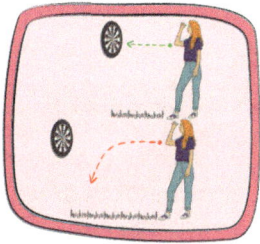 ☐ Set realistic goals.

 ☐ Be clear, sharp, and specific.

 ☐ Get control (as much as possible).

 ☐ Reverse it—start with the endpoint.

 ☐ Break it down (and again, if needed).

 ☐ Make your timeline an essential partner.

 ☐ Give yourself check-up points and follow-ups.

 ☐ Place your plan in front of you and the whole world.

MAKE-IT-HAPPEN TOOL

MY LONG-TERM GOAL

MY SHORT-TERM GOALS	TASKS	CHECK-INS AND FOLLOW-UPS
1		
2		
3		

4		

5		

6		

Helpful Resources for Achieving My Goals

_____

_____

_____

_____

MAKE-IT-HAPPEN TOOL

MY LONG-TERM GOAL

MY SHORT-TERM GOALS	TASKS	CHECK-INS AND FOLLOW-UPS
1		
2		
3		

4		

5		

6		

Helpful Resources for Achieving My Goals

FlyingKids®

SPECIAL GUIDES FOR SPECIAL JOURNEYS

FlyingKids® designs and publishes unique guides for the special journeys in young readers' lives.

Whether exploring countries and cities around the world, or going on a personal journey of self-discovery, young explorers will find FlyingKids' interactive guides always take them on an exciting journey full of fun and special moments.

BE A KID OF THE WORLD

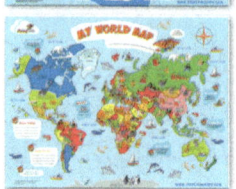

BE WHATEVER YOU WANT, GIRL!

More to come ...

Made in the USA
Las Vegas, NV
26 January 2024

84899191R10046